THE D WORD

sesherlock

ISBN: 9798777312686

Cover design by: sesherlock
Library of Congress Control Number: 2018675309
Printed in the United States of America

To My Baa, where would I be without you?

To FAA, for being the reason for me to keep going.

To UJ, for always encouraging me.

CONTENTS

PREFACE

In this journey from The Darkness back to The Light you will find one more poem in *Recovery* than in *The Darkness*. This symbolises the fact that The Light has always and will always triumph over The Darkness.

INTRODUCTION

Laughter, who's he?

Yes, I knew Joy once but not since she ran off with Confidence though.

Oh, I heard Hope was back for a fleeting visit, didn't pop in on me, mind.

Speaking of mind, I lost her long ago.

Come to think of it it's since the new boss took over.

Really shaken things up.

Tossed out Self-esteem, got rid of friends.

He absolutely does not stand for sleep.

Rationality is a no-no.

Depression he's called.

We call him *The D Word*.

Yep, built himself a whole new headquarters, sacked Faith and has brought in Anxiety instead.

Right jobsworth that one.

On top of that we had a work experience kid, Grief, in.

A two week placement turned into a permanent job.

Supposedly, I manage him but you wouldn't think it.

Kid thinks he owns the place and surprise, surprise the big boss loves him so he'll be around for the foreseeable.

Actually, I lied. Hope did pop in briefly. She was looking for a job but was laughed out the building.

I can't bear my new line manager, Worry. She's a proper micromanager her.

She has to sign off on everything I do. Can't catch a break.

I have zero life outside this job. My social life is DOA and most of my friends have gone.

They see my job is all consuming but can't understand why I let it be.

I wish I could explain it them, to everyone, to the world.

The thing is we all have jobs and every so often we get a sucky new boss.

Resignation is discouraged because the job is so rare and beautiful, even if it's impossible to see sometimes.

We just have to ride it out.

It could be a long old road ahead, but you know who I found cowering in the cleaning cupboard? Belief.

Then we found Trust who had fallen down the back of my desk.

Together we rallied Hope and Confidence, Self-esteem and Positivity.

Strength heard there was a coup and gathered Determination and Motivation in support.

After the longest, most difficult struggle of my life we drove out *The D Word* and Anxiety together.

Not entirely, mind.

They're still lurking in the mailroom and I have no doubt they'll climb the ladder back to the top one day.

It's almost inevitable.

But I know I will always have a team behind me.

They may get lost along the way, but they

never forget their way home.

THE DARKNESS

A thousand enchanting emeralds
illuminate the way
yet the one that didn't shine
is the one that stays.
Hopeless dream
almost but never,
near and dear, gives me fever.
I breathe but I cannot smell,
I read but I cannot tell.
Eyes bleed resentment
blinded by illusive truths.
Pity stained faces all in a row
down, down, down they all fall.
Stabbed where it matters by a
weapon of longing.
Big dreams. Broken dreams. Big bang.
Black hole.

When and where will it all begin?
Crumbling out of my outgrown skin.
Not on the edge, but firmly in the middle.
Supposed to be today not an unborn rid-
dle.

Am I colour blind?
I'm told the sky is blue
but all I see is black.

Am I deaf?
I'm told the birds sing
but all I hear is silence.

Am I alive?
I'm told life is extraordinary
but to me it just feels temporary.

Ashes of a dream
scattered on the waves of disillusion.

The thief time steals my memory.
The jester time wreaks havoc.
The doctor time stitches the wound
And the handyman time papers over
the scars.

I wasn't made for this world.
I can't understand it,
it doesn't understand me.
My brain works differently.
I wasn't made for this world.

People confuse me.
Feelings confuse me.
What's right and what's wrong?
I try to conform,
I try to be what I'm supposed to be,
but my brain just whirls and swirls.
I wasn't made for this world.

I'll never be right,
I'll never understand.
So why continue and grapple
When it's a losing battle?

I wasn't made for this world.

I don't understand the point of me.
I'm good for nothing,
literally.

My soul is weary.
The fire that once raged in the centre of my
being
has long been extinguished.

I wonder if I'll still get wrinkles in my
cheeks
and the corners of my eyes
now that I no longer smile.

There is a wildfire
ravaging my being.
Extinguishing dreams,
leaving ashes of a soul
in its wake.

Sometimes there are no words
to describe the pain, despair, and desper-
ation.
The feeling of no feeling,
numb, like you're under sedation.
Sometimes there are no words.

Sometimes there are no words
to match the misery,
no perfect metaphor or simile.
Sometimes there are no words.

Sometimes there are no words
that will comfort or ease
your weary soul.
No matter hard they try to please,
there's nothing that will bring you in from
the
cold.
Sometimes there are no words.

Sometimes there are no words.
Sometimes the deafening silence is all you
can hear.

The blinding darkness making it impossible to steer

your way to the light.

And the strait jacket of agony making it
impossible

to fight

clear

of the omnipresent fog.

Sometimes there are no words.

Sometimes all there is to do is cry,
but the tears won't flow and I don't know
why.

I sit not in silence, but a haze of white
noise.
Numb to all feeling, so delicately poised.

Inside I'm drowning. Inside I can't
breathe.
Outside I fake a smile, broken and un-
sheathed.

I want to scream, to cry, to fight,
to flail, to kick, to howl, to bite.
To punch, to sob, to scratch
with all my might.

I can't even get that right.

One minute I was floating
the next I was sinking.
At first I struggled, tried to fight the tide.
I thought I was safe.
They lied.
I was sinking.
Deep, deep, and deeper still.
The cold rising, the light fading.
Dark, dark, and darker still.
Murky waters.
Shadows invading
my head, my heart, my mind.
My mind. My mind? My…
I've lost my mind.

I've been in the depths so long
my eyes no longer recall the light.
Everything once so right,
now wrong.
The beauty of day hidden by night.

What was warm is now cold
what was young is now old.
What brought joy now festers
like rotting mould.

I fell apart.

I tore my skin hoping it would all leak out, the scars just sealed it in.

I cried, I punched, I fought and I crumbled.

I bled despair, breathed in hopelessness and exhaled all I was.

I ran, I sweated, I curled up and hid my face.

The brightest days were the darkest days.

It's been a minute now since the sun last
came up
and I'm kind of getting used to the dark.
I see shadows now that weren't there be-
fore
and the chill in the air is stark.

Somebody please help me.
I can't breathe
I can't breathe.
My chest is collapsing
And it feels like a hundred degrees.
I claw at my skin in the hopes I might feel
the pain, the air, the scars,
anything real.
But I can't breathe,
I can't breathe.
Somebody please help me.
The air is dry, my mouth a dune.
I can't see, I can't breathe
get me out of this room
where the walls are caving in.

What do I want, what do I need?
I bleed I bleed I bleed.
A kind thought, a good deed
I bleed I bleed I bleed.
I stay, I bleed.
I flee, I bleed.
Selfish stubborn greed
I bleed
I bleed.
Into the wild flames she leads,
And I bleed, I bleed.
Desperate tired pleas
I bleed.
Stuck between the boggy reeds
I bleed.
At home amongst the weeds
I bleed.
Until I am freed
I bleed.

The shoebox under my bed
is where my caged heart flies free.
Home to the contents of a heavy soul,
a blink, a glance, a memory.

Old memories hold hands and
dance to the rhythm of my hungry heart.
Snapshots of a life past
and a love lost.

My smiles and tears seek the light
of another day.
My soul mourns its missing piece
hidden away.

Elation and terror make friends
and play
feeding on my heart once
so well fed
in the shoebox under my bed.

Year by year, neatly tied with string.
Once familiar faces and foreign lands.
Once homely truths, now aged reminis-
cences,

A hidden land.

Remember, forget, hold close
or let loose.
Wake to yesterday and shut the curtains
on
tomorrow?

Or flourish and bloom
in a life well led.
And leave the dusty shoebox under my
bed.

My graduation picture sits facing the wall.
I haven't been able to look at it for four
years now.
It reminds me of all the things I should
have achieved,
the life I should have had, the career.
I hope one day I can look at it,
maybe even be proud.
Look back and be pleased
with all the things I have become.
But until that day falls
my graduation picture sits facing the wall.

Pain, pain
go away,
Don't come back another day.

I just want to feel again.
To see again, to believe again.
To breathe again.

I just want to feel again
without the current choking me.
I want music to awaken my dormant soul
and the magic of this world to drag me out
of this hole.

I want to smile and mean it.
I want my eyes to drink in the sunsets
and my heart to beat without regrets.

I just want to feel again.

To all the friends I lost along the way,
I'm sorry, I miss you,
I long for you every day.

I want to go home.

Home, where music soothes my bones
and awakens my emotions.
Home, to my mother's arms and uncondi-
tional devotion.

I want to go home to my father's hands,
my brother's protection.
My sister's intelligence and integrity,
my nieces' unassuming innocence.

I want to go home to my sister in law's un-
wavering resilience,
my brother in law's kindness and courage.
Home, to the warmth and certainty of the
sun
Home, where I will never be alone.

I want the moon to illuminate the stars
and gently guide me home.

I want to say thank you to my mum
because all I am is down to her.
But that would be an insult to her
to say
she made me this way.
It's not her fault that I'm not good for
much
that I can't get anything right.
It's not because of her that I fell down this
hole
and can no longer recall the light.
I thank her for not giving up on me
even when I make things harder.
For still believing I'm worth something
with all her strength and ardour.
So I won't thank you for all that I am
But
for the fact that
I still am
at all.

RECOVERY

When I woke up this morning I heard the
sun calling through my window
and resting on my face.
When I opened my eyes I saw colours in
what, for so long, had been an empty
space.

Many trees and plants only bloom for just a few weeks in a year. The rest of the year is spent going back underground and getting to know its roots again. Feeding, absorbing the rain, resting and preparing. Re-growing, ready to bloom again. We musn't pressure ourselves to be at our best all the time. Not only is it ok, but it is necessary to retreat underground to rest and get to know ourselves again. Don't be alarmed when you feel yourself wilting, it is your body beginning the process of rejuvenation and it is wholly natural.

There are dark, cold, wet days when it feels
as though Spring will never return.

Leaves block doorways and you think
you'll never see through the mist on the
window pane.

Pane? Pain.

Then, amongst the sodden soil,

the tiniest green shoot breaks through the
frost.

Spring is on its way.

Spring always returns.

Remember that flowers need the rain in order to bloom at their best and thrive.
In fact, they need it to survive.
A perfect balance of rain and sun.
Too much of either will kill it.
Enjoy the sun and embrace the rain for they are both giving you life.

All plants need deadheading in order to keep blooming.

So do you and I.

If we go season on season carrying the same dead weight,

not only will we not bloom again, we'll die.

Truth is your only real friend in this life.
Keep her close.

Don't be afraid to begin again.
I lost myself and mourned her for so long
until I realised I could be
new and better.
Stronger and fiercer.

Remember the night sky looks its best when the lights are off.
Don't be afraid of the dark.

Wrap your pain in something soft
and pop it somewhere safe.
In years to come you'll find it
and be reminded of
How Far You've Come.

Don't shut out the pain.

Embrace it, feel it, allow it to flood your being.

It will forever be a part of you.

Don't shun it, or shame it

Take pride in it, name it.

It is as much a part of you as the freckle on your right hand.

Close your eyes. Breathe. Repeat.

Don't ever allow yourself to feel as though your pain doesn't matter or isn't valid.
That is a dangerous trap.
Your pain is relative to you and should never be compared to anyone else's.
You are valid.
You matter.
You deserve to be listened to, helped,
Loved.
You Matter.

Just close your eyes and take a moment.
Remember how rare and extraordinary
this life is.
A miracle. Each and every one.

Pain is the frenemy we love to hate.
Annoying, self-indulgent and turns up
when it's least welcome.
But, as much as we hate to admit it,
we know we're
Stronger, Better, Fiercer
for having him around.

The girl I had mourned for so long had never gone away.

She was simply waiting for me in the woman I would become.

I lost.

I lost purpose.

I lost worth and reason.

I lost myself.

But I never lost hope.

And all of a sudden,
out of the darkness,
the moon scooped me up
and cradled me in her arms.
"I'll take care of you," she whispered.
"Until the sun returns."

Suddenly I'm awake.
My eyes open, gone the ache
of yesterday.
My dormant lungs now thirsty for air
to breathe, and feel, and be
again.

I'm rising and floating and
smiling and swimming and
dreaming.
I'm here. I'm still here.
There! The light.
I'm stretching, grabbing, clawing, clasping
"Where have you been?" I can hear the
light asking.
So warm and fresh.
An old friend.
My rejuvenated arms full of colours and
tastes and scents.
And hope.
I'm floating again.

Hope is your first breath in the morning when breathing is the last thing on your mind.

Hope is the rain rapping on your window and wind whispering from behind.

It is the promise of the morning sun and the omnipresent moonlight.

As sure as lambs and daffodils in spring.

Your mother's arms, your father's hands.

Hope is remembering. Always remembering.

Taking your pain and wrapping it in memory. A shoebox under your bed.

Hope is your life tucked in your pocket for keeping, remembering, crying, smiling, breathing.

A new day.

A few of my favourite things.

Freshly cut grass. The smell of my mother. Tears on my cheeks reminding me I'm alive. Veins. Drinks with friends. Dinner with family. A hot bath followed by clean jamies and climbing into fresh, clean sheets. Blue suits and brown shoes. Fresh faces. That one warm, old, comfy jumper. Pet snuggles. Exercise. Everything about my mum. My sister's teeth. My sister's legs. My sister's wardrobe! Music. All music. Art. Real, honest people. Unexpected friends. Honesty. The sun. Perfect blue skies. Cold, starry nights. Running in the rain. My mum's cooking. Cheese. The permanent watch tan on my dad's wrist. My teddy. A good pen. My protective brother. Genuine smiles. Genuine people. The moon. Soul mates. The Ocean. Swimming. Red pandas. Quokkas. Penguins. Elephants. ALL baby animals. Guilt free lie ins. Using my brain. Completing a job well. Drawing. Curly hair on boys. My first breath in the morning. Luck of literacy. Laughing until my tummy hurts. Making other people laugh. Giving gifts. My beautiful nieces. Old souls. Young souls. Sensitivity. Strength. Women. Men who respect women. People who follow their dreams. 'Me' time. Poetry. Old intimacy with new friends. Possibility. Hope. A better future.

My seams came away
and I fell apart.
But my nieces sewed me
back together.

I found myself in the gutter with Oscar
but I couldn't see the stars.
I lay the wrong way,
my face in the mud
the dirt seeping into my scars.

But as I started to give up,
giving myself to the earth
I heard a gentle voice behind me
whispering my worth.

I heard a thud in my ear
boomboom boomboom
My heart.
It's still beating.
So this isn't a tomb?

I turned towards the voice
and I saw several faces.
Those of my mother and siblings,
their partners, and my nieces.

I heard Oscar giggle,
a giggle of triumph.
"You thought I meant the stars in the sky",

He laughed.

"The stars are all around you,

You just have to open your eyes."

I wasn't prepared for the storm
and I nearly drowned in the flood.
But I found my defences; my family.
They've given me the equipment to defend
against the storm.
My nieces are my umbrella in the rain,
my mother and siblings the sandbags at
the door.
I'm protected now.
For when the next storm comes.

.

Dear FAA,
I hope you always feel loved
because I can promise you that you are
and ALWAYS will be.
I hope you never feel you don't matter
because to your family you are *all* that
matters.
I hope when you feel afraid, you know it
won't last
and you never get stuck
in the unchangeable past.
I hope you remember
it WILL improve
even when you feel so far removed
from everything that matters.
I hope you take the time to know yourselves
and love yourselves
even when your mind constantly rebels.
I hope you never have to face the dark
but know that if you do
you won't be alone
because your family will be the light

that guides you home.

Sat on my bench,
a heavy mist disguising the horizon,
a palpable chill piercing my skin,
an autumn bonfire invading my senses.
Not far from the road,
yet silence.
The naked trees mutely observing
the stillness
hanging like rags on a line.
Then
a discreet rustle
and a crescendoing chirp.
Then another.
Twittering and tweeting and singing
overhaul the rusty air.
A whip of wind uncovers a cowering cro-
cus
from under the burnt, crusty leaves.
Signs of life
even on the dreariest of days.

It's always there
under the leaves,

swinging in the trees.
High in the sky,
far and nigh.
Life.

The sun will rise again.
The plants will bud,
the grass will grow.
The trees will sprout,
the birds will crow.
And you, my dear, will see it all.
Just hold on.

Printed in Great Britain
by Amazon

79228651R00041